PEOPLE OF CHARACTER

George Washington

A Life of Self-discipline

Written by Anne Todd
Illustrated by Tina Walski

BLASTOFF!
4
READERS

Note to Librarians, Teachers, and Parents:

Blastoff! Readers are carefully developed by literacy experts and combine standards-based content with developmentally-appropriate text.

Level 1 provides the most support through repetition of high-frequency words, light text, predictable sentence patterns, and strong visual support.

Level 2 offers early readers a bit more challenge through varied simple sentences, increased text load, and less repetition of high frequency words.

Level 3 advances early-fluent readers toward fluency through increased text and concept load, less reliance on visuals, longer sentences, and more literary language.

Level 4 builds reading stamina by providing more text per page, increased use of punctuation, greater variation in sentence patterns, and increasingly challenging vocabulary.

Level 5 encourages children to move from "learning to read" to "reading to learn" by providing even more text, varied writing styles, and less familiar topics.

Whichever book is right for your reader, Blastoff! Readers are the perfect books to build confidence and encourage a love of reading that will last a lifetime!

This edition first published in 2008 by Bellwether Media.

No part of this publication may be reproduced in whole or in part without written permission of the publisher. For information regarding permission, write to Bellwether Media Inc., Attention: Permissions Department, Post Office Box 1C, Minnetonka, MN 55345-9998.

Library of Congress Cataloging-in-Publication Data
Todd, Anne M.
  George Washington : a life of self-discipline / by Anne Todd.
    p. cm. – (Blastoff! readers : people of character)
Summary: "People of character explores important character traits through the lives of famous historical figures. George Washington highlights how this great individual demonstrated self-discipline during his life. Intended for grades three through six"–Provided by publisher.
  Includes bibliographical references and index.
  ISBN-13: 978-1-60014-094-5 (hardcover : alk. paper)
  ISBN-10: 1-60014-094-7 (hardcover : alk. paper)
  1. Washington, George, 1732–1799–Juvenile literature. 2. Self-control–United States–Juvenile literature. 3. Presidents–United States–Biography–Juvenile literature. I. Title.

E312.66.T63 2008
973.4'1092–dc22
  [B]   2007019691

Contents

Have you ever worked hard toward a goal? Was it harder to achieve than you expected? If you kept working toward your goal even when it was tough, then you have self-discipline. Self-discipline helps you do and be your best. It helps you get things done. It can also help you become a leader. George Washington was a great American leader with true self-discipline.

George was born on a farm
in Virginia in 1732. He spent
his childhood working on the
farm and going to school.
He always worked hard.
At age 16, George took a job
surveying lands in Virginia.
He took his work seriously and
saved the money he earned.

When George was young, **Great Britain** ruled thirteen **colonies** along the eastern coast of America. During that time, European explorers were claiming new lands to the west of the colonies. In the 1750s, Great Britain and France fought a war over control of the new lands. The war was called the **French and Indian War**.

George joined the Virginia **militia** and fought hard and bravely for Great Britain. He became the leader of the militia and helped lead Great Britain to victory.

George returned to farming after the war. He and his wife Martha lived on a farm in Virginia called Mount Vernon. George's self-discipline helped him become very successful. He enjoyed life on his farm. But in 1775, the American colonies needed his help.

Tension was growing between the American colonists and Great Britain. The **British** King had made many laws that angered the colonists. He placed taxes on their supplies. He did not allow them to settle in certain areas. The colonists wanted to make their own decisions. They did not want Great Britain to control them. Many wanted a **revolution**. They needed a leader. George accepted the call to lead this **Revolutionary War**.

The British had a large army, good weapons, plenty of supplies, and well-trained soldiers. The colonists did not. But they had a great leader.

George worked hard and his self-discipline set an example for his soldiers. He led several successful attacks on the British.

The British won many
battles in the following
years of the war. Life was
hard for the American
troops. They were often
hungry, tired, and cold.
But, following George's
example, they did not
lose hope. Soon they
began winning battles.

Finally, George led his troops to victory! The colonies were free from British rule! Some people thought George would become king. Others, including George, believed laws should govern people, not kings.

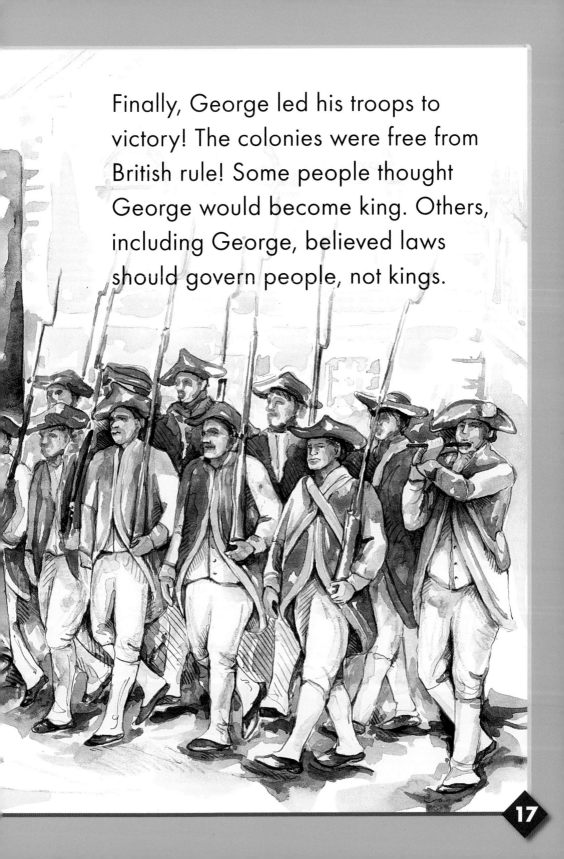

George returned to work on his farm. But around him, he saw a **government** that lacked unity. He supported colonial leaders who thought the country needed a **constitution**. With George's support, the colonial leaders met and wrote the Constitution of the United States of America. They then elected George the first President of the United States.

George served two **terms** as President. When he left office he wanted to spend his final years with Martha at Mount Vernon. He died in 1799. Americans named the capital city **Washington, D.C.**, and built the Washington monument to honor him. His self-discipline and hard work helped create a free and united country.

Glossary

British—of Great Britain

colonies—territories settled by people under rule from their home country

constitution—the system of principles that govern a nation

French and Indian War—the war in America in which France and its Indian allies fought against England (1754-1760)

government—a system of control and direction for a group of people

Great Britain—an island in Europe made up of England, Scotland, and Wales

militia—the military force of each colony

revolution—the overthrow of a government

Revolutionary War—the war for American independence from Great Britain (1775-1783)

surveying—to determine the boundaries of an area of land

terms—measured amounts of time

Washington, D.C.—the capital city of the United States of America; D.C. stands for District of Columbia, the area of land that makes up the city.

To Learn More

AT THE LIBRARY
Calkhoven, Laurie. *George Washington: An American Life*. New York: Sterling, 2007.

Heilbroner, Joan. *Meet George Washington*. New York: Random House, 2001.

January, Brendan. *George Washington: America's 1st President*. New York: Children's Press, 2003.

ON THE WEB
Learning more about George Washington is as easy as 1, 2, 3.

1. Go to www.factsurfer.com

2. Enter "George Washington" into search box.

3. Click the "Surf" button and you will see a list of related web sites.

With factsurfer.com, finding more information is just a click away.

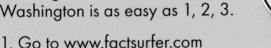

Index